# On Southern Lines

## Roy Hobbs

First published 1997

ISBN 0 7110 2462 6

Published by Ian Allan Publishing

An imprint of Ian Allan Ltd, Terminal House, Station Approach, Shepperton, Surrey TW17 8AS; and printed by Ian Allan Printing Ltd, at its works at Coombelands in Runneymede, Surrey.

Code: 9708/C

*Front Cover:*
Urie 'H15' class 4-6-0 No 30491 is depicted leaving Hinton Admiral station on the main line between Southampton and Bournemouth on 29 June 1957. One of the many camping coaches distributed throughout the region at that time can just be discerned behind the rearmost carriage. *R.C. Riley*

*Right:*
Pictured west of Wilton is well-groomed 'Merchant Navy' class Pacific No 35017 *Belgian Marine* with an SLS Special on 23 May 1965. This had originated at Birmingham, travelling via Reading and Salisbury to Exeter and thence returning via Taunton, Westbury and Bristol to Birmingham. Light Pacific No 34051 *Winston Churchill* had been employed on the initial stage, being changed at Salisbury for No 35017 which ran as far as Westbury.

*All uncredited photos taken by the author.*

*Above:*
Typical of the many branch lines operating in Southern territory was that from
Three Bridges to East Grinstead. Here former SECR 'H' class 0-4-4T No 31518,
coupled to its Maunsell twin-coach push-pull set, is seen leaving Rowfant with a
train in the latter direction on a wintry day in February 1963. The line survived into
the dieselisation era, being integrated into the Oxted lines scheme employing
three-car DEMUs in June 1963.

# Introduction

The Southern Railway at the Grouping of 1923 was formed of three main constituents. These were the South Eastern & Chatham Railway (SECR), resulting from the 1899 amalgamation of two rival companies, the South Eastern Railway (SER) and London, Chatham & Dover Railway (LCDR), which covered the greater part of Kent and intruded into East Sussex; the London, Brighton & South Coast Railway (LBSCR) serving most of rural Surrey and Sussex; and the largest, the London & South Western Railway (LSWR) whose extensive territory ranged from urban Surrey and Hampshire in the east, through Dorset to mid-Devon and North Cornwall in the west, and included connections with the Isle of Wight.

In preparing this title the intention has been to provide a broad view of the operations of its successor, the Southern Region of British Railways, in the late 1950s and 1960s, before the elimination of steam traction took effect in July 1967. For this reason a variety of aspects has been covered, from branch line to express passenger working; from visits of normally foreign locomotives through to enthusiast railtours, together with the occasional locomotive shed view.

Despite being the smallest of the 'Big Four' companies prior to Nationalisation, the Southern was still distinctive at this time in possessing a significant number of pre-Grouping locomotives, even though an extensive programme of electrification had already been undertaken, and plans were already under way for its further development. But for the intervention of World War 2, and subsequent Nationalisation, these would, no doubt, have been implemented, considerably altering the railway as we know it. Although large schemes such as the South Eastern and Bournemouth programmes eventually came into effect, it seems likely that further lines, some now closed, such as on the former LBSCR system for example, would also have received the benefits provided by such modernisation, including regular and frequent interval services. As a result of the considerable electrification that had already taken place, the old company had already received the rather unkind description of the 'tram track'.

However, one could in the postwar era still discover various elderly tank or tender locomotives operating on branch and secondary lines across the system from Kent to Cornwall, and it was only with the advent of various Standard types in the 1950s that changes slowly began to make themselves felt, in certain cases only a few years before steam traction was ultimately eliminated.

On the main lines, services had been subject to improvement, following the end of hostilities, by the introduction of Bulleid's unconventional 'Merchant Navy' 4-6-2s and lighter sister engines of the virtually identical 'West Country' and 'Battle of Britain' classes, these being used extensively throughout the region.

As mentioned earlier, some attempt has been made to present a wide selection of Southern activities during the period mentioned, which will, I hope, help most readers recall a time when so much variety and interest still existed. Picture order has been organised basically from east to west, with occasional variation, taking each of the main routes of the original pre-Grouping companies radiating from London and in turn incorporating the various associated branch lines depicted.

## Bibliography

F. Burtt: *SECR Locomotives;* Ian Allan.
F. Burtt: *LBSCR Locomotives;* Ian Allan.
F. Burtt: *LSWR Locomotives;* Ian Allan.
W. Philip Connolly: *British Railways Pre-Grouping Atlas and Gazetteer;* Ian Allan.
G. Daniels & L. A. Dench: *Passengers No More;* Ian Allan.
H. P. White: *Regional History of the Railways of Great Britain; Vols 1-3;* David & Charles.
Other Publications: The various series published by the Middleton Press profiling the railways of Southern England.
Society Journals: *LCGB Bulletin, Railway Observer* (RCTS).
Magazines: *Backtrack; Modern Railways; Railway Magazine; Railway World; Trains Illustrated.*

## Acknowledgements

To fill the gaps in my own collection, especially in the Kent and southwest areas, I have had to rely on contributions from the collections of other photographers, these being credited where appropriate. I would offer my particular thanks for their assistance and kindness in allowing the use of now valuable and irreplaceable transparencies, which I hope will help present a balanced view of operations over the time concerned.

*Roy Hobbs*
Feniton
Devon

*Above:* Against the background of a changing London, rebuilt 'West Country' class Pacific No 34021 *Dartmoor* is seen leaving Charing Cross with the down 'Man of Kent' on 25 July 1959.  *C.J. Gammell*

*Right:* Cannon Street station, with its roof still intact, is host to the then new DEMU No 1017, built for services between London and Hastings whilst rebuilt 'West Country' class Pacific No 34025 *Whimple* awaits

departure with a Kent express on 31 May 1958. This station, built in 1866 for the SER, still experiences considerable commuter traffic on weekdays, being situated in the heart of the City of London.  *R.C. Riley*

*Left:* The 12.44pm Ramsgate van train is seen here leaving London Bridge with Maunsell rebuild 'D1' class 4-4-0 No 31735 in charge on 14 May 1959. St Paul's Cathedral is visible in the background with several now-disappeared dockside cranes that once lined the many active wharves serving this area of the Thames, later abandoned to commercial operation. Somewhat unusually the former SECR upper level through lines towards Cannon Street and Charing Cross appear to be devoid of trains on this occasion. Out of sight, on the extreme left, are the remaining terminal platforms which served trains on the ex-LBSCR section, these originating mainly from Sussex and south coast resorts. As many other London termini, the station has been completely remodelled and rebuilt during recent years, showing little evidence of its former shabby and rambling nature, probably, in part, the result of enemy action during World War 2. London Bridge, the oldest London terminal, had its origins in the London & Greenwich Railway, initially opened between Deptford and Spa Road, west of Bermondsey, during February 1836. The line was extended first to London Bridge in December 1836 and later from Deptford to Greenwich in May 1838. *R.C. Riley*

*Above:* Passing Denmark Hill with a down relief for the Kent coast on 14 May 1959 is Maunsell 'Schools' class 4-4-0 No 30936 *Cranleigh*. The station was operated jointly in pre-Grouping days by the LCDR and LBSCR, the left-hand tracks being the first to be electrified in December 1909 by the latter company. These were originally on the 6,700V ac overhead system, which remained in use until June 1928, and formed part of the South London line between Victoria and London Bridge. The station buildings were severely damaged by fire in 1980, but were subsequently restored as licensed premises following local pressure. *R.C. Riley*

*Above:* This view, taken at Shepherdswell on 23 May 1959, depicts former SECR 'L' class 4-4-0 No 31768 arriving on a Faversham to Dover local with Set 454 comprising Maunsell narrow-bodied stock designed for routes with restricted clearances, especially that between Tonbridge and Hastings. These 22 engines were known colloquially as 'Germans', 10 being constructed in Germany by the manufacturer Borsig, the last to be built being delivered immediately before World War 1. One of the class, originally A763, was unofficially named *Betty Baldwin* by a wartime volunteer driver, the name being painted on the leading splashers, and it was assumed to be the name of the lady with whom he was romantically linked. The last example was withdrawn in December 1961, but not before an official attempt to restore one for special duties was unfortunately abandoned earlier that year. Shepherdswell was notable as being a terminus of the once independent East Kent Railway. The last section, to Tilmanstone Colliery (on its Eastry line), closed with the Kent coalfield run-down in the mid-1980s.

*R.C. Riley*

*Right:* Designed by Harry Wainwright, Locomotive Superintendent of the former SECR, 'C' class 0-6-0 No 31481 engages in a shunting movement at Shepherdswell station on the same date as the previous picture. Engines of this class, eventually totalling 108, were the workhorses of the railway, being used equally on both local passenger and freight duties. Withdrawal of the final three examples, which ended their days as Ashford Works shunters was completed by November 1966, the last, No 31592, now being preserved on the Bluebell Railway.

*T.B. Owen*

9

*Left:* Unrebuilt 'Battle of Britain' Class 4-6-2 No 34078 *222 Squadron* passes the unusual signalbox at Kearnsey Loop Junction on 23 May 1959 with duty 474, an afternoon working from Charing Cross to Ramsgate. The junction loop, seen diverging right towards Canterbury, was constructed by the LCDR and opened in July 1882, in order to compete with the rival SER for traffic to Deal. To stifle this competition the latter threatened initially that access to its Deal station would be refused! In later years the loop saw little use other than for military traffic during both World Wars, and also in early 1953 when the North Kent coastal lines experienced flood damage. The loop was subsequently taken out of use, the box itself closing in December 1980. *T.B. Owen*

*Above:* Work-stained examples of 'C' class 0-6-0s Nos 31721 and 31724 together with an unidentified Maunsell Mogul, contrast with a diminutive 204hp diesel shunter in Ashford shed yard on 25 February 1962. Ashford was the main works of the SECR, being responsible for major overhauls of those classes originating on their system until 1962 when all work was transferred to Eastleigh.

BR Standard Class 4MT 2-6-4T No 80031 heads the line-up outside Ashford shed on 15 October 1961, consisting of two Class C 0-6-0s, the breakdown unit, a 350hp diesel shunter and 'W' class 2-6-4T. The BR Standard '4MT' 2-6-4Ts arrived on the Region from December 1959 when they were exchanged for several similar Brighton-built LMR-designed 2-6-4Ts, that were allocated to replace the various pre-Grouping passenger classes such as the former LBSCR Class I3 4-4-2Ts. This became necessary in the postwar period where heavier trains, especially those on London commuter services, had resulted in the need for more appropriate modern power. The Standards lasted until the end of steam on the Southern Region during 1967.

Appropriately garlanded former SECR 'O1' class 0-6-0 No 31065, by this time the last representative of its type, together with 'C' class 0-6-0 No 31592, wait at the end of Paddock Wood platform on 11 July 1961 to take over the stock of their LCGB special from London, before proceeding down the Hawkhurst branch with the last train before closure. This was, in fact, the final day of steam over the South Eastern section of the Southern Region before electrification.

No 31065, although modified by replacement of its domeless boiler, was in 1961 the last existing example of James Stirling's designs for the SER and still retained its then unique outside sprung tender. Both engines have fortunately survived into the preservation era. The 'O1' class was a rebuild by Wainwright of the earlier 'O' class which had been constructed between 1878 and 1899. From 1903 until 1927 a programme was undertaken to alter some 58 engines, nearly half

the original class. The main differences were the installation of a new cab, domed boiler with increased pressure and fitment of steam sanding gear together with vacuum brake. At the end of steam power on the SE section only two engines survived, Nos 31065 and 31258. These had been retained to work the lightly laid track of the former East Kent Railway between Shepherdswell and Tilmanstone Colliery.

*Left:* Former 'H' class 0-4-4T No 31519 stands at Dunton Green with a two-coach push-pull set destined for Westerham on 20 March 1960. This branch had been the subject of earlier attempts at closure, these being thwarted by the local TUCC, who stated that considerable inconvenience and hardship would be caused to the local commuting public. However, the Transport Minister, Ernest Marples, then visited the railway, reportedly in dark glasses, and subsequently announced '......it would be cheaper to provide all passengers with a motor scooter!', so overruling their decision. The closed line was itself the subject of an early preservation attempt, and Westerham station buildings, together with the signalbox, were even painted with this end in view. Unfortunately, the scheme foundered owing to a section being required for the now infamous M25 motorway.    *C.J. Gammell*

*Above:* Westerham terminus is shown here with 'H' class 0-4-4T No 31324 departing with a working to Dunton Green on 27 May 1961. Set 610 was one of several using converted coaches of Maunsell design, usually comprising open third and corridor brake coaches, which were introduced in the early 1960s to replace the many sets of pre-Grouping origin, one being illustrated opposite, used on the majority of Southern branches up to that time.    *T.B. Owen*

*Above:* BR Standard Class 4MT No 80142 arrives at Edenbridge on the Tonbridge to Redhill route of the former SECR with a local train for the latter destination in May 1963. Until the advent of BR Standard designs, the line had mainly been the territory of various 4-4-0s of pre-Grouping origin, along with the Maunsell 2-6-0s, usually of Class N. These continued to serve the line alongside the BR 2-6-4Ts until replacement by DEMUs in January 1965. The buildings shown here were demolished in June 1971, being replaced by the usual nondescript brick shelter. The locality was also served by Edenbridge Town station on the former LBSCR Oxted to Tunbridge Wells West line, although this was about a mile distant. Electrification of the route on the third-rail system was completed in May 1994.

*Right:* Passing its distinctly ornate signalbox in June 1963, 'N' class 2-6-0 No 31411 approaches Nutfield station with a stopping train between Redhill and Tonbridge. The local chemical company's siding can be seen trailing away from the up line immediately to the rear of the box, which is of similar architectural design to that located at Sandling on the line between Ashford and Folkestone.

NUTFIELD

31411

WARNING
STOP LOOK & LISTEN
BEFORE CROSSING THE LINE

WARNING
STOP LOOK & LISTEN
BEFORE CROSSING THE LINE

*Left:* A rather unkempt multiple blastpipe fitted 'Schools' class 4-4-0, probably No 30907 *Dulwich*, makes a spirited departure from Redhill with the Tunbridge Wells section of the 5.25pm London Bridge to Reading commuter train in May 1961. This train and its related up working represented a long-standing tradition, being the last normal regular steam-hauled passenger service between London and Redhill, latterly for a period being worked by Bulleid Light Pacifics of the 'West Country' and 'Battle of Britain' classes, and occasionally double-headed, usually by a Maunsell Mogul. The service had origins dating back to pre-Grouping times. With the rundown of steam, final elimination took place on 18 February 1963 when substitution was made by an EMU running from London Bridge to Reigate only, ongoing passengers having to change on to the existing local service.

*Above:* Maunsell 'U1' class, three-cylindered 2-6-0 No 31891 emerges from the north end of Redhill tunnel on the Quarry line, avoiding Redhill, with an inter-regional holiday train on 22 July 1961. The headcode indicates a working to the LMR via the West London line. The leading coach is a WR Hawksworth brake corridor vehicle, identified by its distinctive roof end profile. These summer through coastal workings were mainly withdrawn during the early 1960s.

*Below:* The time is around 8.30am on 6 June 1962 and WR '43XX' class 2-6-0 No 6337 has just arrived at Redhill with the 6.50am Reading to Redhill service. As commuters hurry to make connection with the adjoining electric unit for London, military personnel, probably having completed basic training at the various camps served by North Camp station, alight to make their way on to an initial posting. This train was invariably hauled on weekdays by either a Class 43XX 2-6-0 or latterly, 'Manor' class 4-6-0. For a short period during the 1950s a WR Class 61XX 2-6-2T was tried experimentally but found to be unsatisfactory. This particular daily working continued, presumably to maintain WR crew familiarity with the route, as at the height of the summer, Saturday services from the Midlands were worked by these men.

*Right:* On a cold and misty morning in early December 1963, Christmas parcels workings at Redhill, a major postal distribution centre, are in full swing. Maunsell 'Q' class 0-6-0 No 30541, now preserved, unhitches several vans from the train occupying Platform 3 before transferring them to the GPO sorting office bay. In the meantime an up Brighton to London parcels special waits for the road on Platform 2.

On a beautifully sunny Sunday morning in June 1963 Willesden (1A) MPD's former LMS Class 5 4-6-0 No 45379 passes Redhill on the down through line with a inter-regional excursion to the south coast. This particular working was unusual, such excursions normally using the Redhill avoiding line, which must have been under maintenance on this occasion. The locomotive is also of interest having been a resident of the well-known Barry graveyard following withdrawal from traffic in July 1965 and subsequently being rescued for preservation. It is currently undergoing restoration at the Bitton on the Avon Valley Railway.

With Redhill 'B' box, now demolished, in the background, Maunsell 'Q' class 0-6-0 No 30543, fitted with a Standard chimney, engages in shunting movements in the up yard sidings in April 1964. Such a scene was untypical at this time, a 350hp diesel shunter normally being employed on these duties. The 'Q' class, which eventually totalled some 20 engines, had been introduced in 1938 as a replacement for the many pre-Grouping 0-6-0 types, which existed throughout the system. From the outset they were found to suffer from steaming difficulties, as a result of which several of the class were modified by Bulleid with the Lemaitre multiple-jet blast pipe and large diameter chimney. This did not, however, prove to be the complete solution and, following draughting experiments carried out on No 30549 in 1955, a number of the class were, from 1958 onwards, fitted with a modified blastpipe and standard chimney of BR design. The result was a much more efficient locomotive, in which most of the previous problems had been overcome. Redhill 'B' box officially closed in May 1985.

*Left:* Former SR 'U1' class 2-6-0 No 31895 waits in the down through road at Redhill in December 1962 with a southbound Christmas parcels working. Vans are presumably being detached at the rear for transfer to the GPO sorting bay. The 204hp diesel shunter has possibly been drafted in to assist with the extra traffic.

*Above:* Redhill shed hosts a trio of Maunsell 'U' and 'N' class 2-6-0s in October 1964. These, including the 'U1' class were synonymous with the shed over a long period of time, including the postwar period up to the early 1960s, and one such example, No 31850, was actually broken up there towards the end of steam

working in January 1965. No 31405, just backing off the coaling stage, retains its Maunsell chimney, whilst the two 'U Boats' have been modified with the standard type. No 31791 has also been provided with altered front-end arrangements under a programme initiated by Ashford around 1955 to improve overall performance.

Betchworth station, on the Redhill to Guildford line, receives an unusual visitor on 23 September 1964, in the shape of former LMS 'Black 5' 4-6-0 No 45346 on the 4.4pm Redhill to Reading service. This engine had worked the Newcastle to Newhaven car sleeper train on 10 September and subsequently failed. Following return to Redhill, its usual stabling point, the necessary repairs were carried out and this view shows it on a running-in turn. The station was one of those suggested for closure after the 1963 Beeching Plan proposals to withdraw all passenger services from the line were rejected. Fortunately, local opposition prevented this action being taken, and it is currently operational, the present lifting barriers being remotely controlled, as elsewhere. The siding nearest the camera at one time served the systems of the Dorking Greystone Lime Co, which, until 1960, operated locomotives on both standard and narrow gauges. The majority of these were unique and of considerable antiquity, dating from the late 19th century. Most have now been preserved at various sites throughout the country.

An unidentified former GWR '43XX' class 2-6-0 drifts down Gomshall bank, at the foot of the North Downs ridge, towards Dorking with an inter-regional train in September 1962. This was a recognised test for train crews in the Guildford direction, with a gradient of 1 in 96 for over three miles. These engines were almost totally responsible for such working throughout the 1950s and early 1960s, until their general reduction in 1963/4 resulted in the 'Manor' class 4-6-0s' being substituted. The latter then continued, virtually without exception, on the daily duty from Reading to Redhill, up to the replacement of steam traction in January 1965. The route was originally part of the Reading, Guildford & Reigate Railway, incorporated in 1846 to build some 46 miles between Reading and Reigate (later Redhill). The first sections to open were Redhill to Dorking and Reading to Farnborough in July 1849. The former was extended to Shalford in August 1849, the LSWR opening its Guildford to Ash Junction section on the same date, giving its rival running powers and enabling services to be run from Reading to Guildford. The final link was completed in October 1849, the LSWR's new Guildford-Godalming section providing running powers to Shalford Junction.

*Left:* In a view taken from the train, shed pilot 'USA' class 0-6-0T No 30072, currently preserved on the Worth Valley Railway in West Yorkshire, stands alongside Guildford shed on 27 July 1963, awaiting its next turn of duty. This replaced one of the former LSWR 'B4' class 0-4-0Ts previously allocated, in much the same manner as the class had taken the place of 'B4s' in Southampton Docks in the immediate postwar period. Guildford shed at this time was host to several Maunsell 2-6-0s, some of which can be observed around the site. The depot ceased operation on 9 July 1967 and the whole area, including the coal stage, seen in the distance on the right hand side, has become the Farnham Road Car Park, a large multi-storey block having been built on the shed site.

*Above:* Seen here leaving Guildford in October 1964 with a Redhill bound train is BR Standard Class 5 No 73050. This loco was on loan from Shrewsbury (6D) MPD, to cover a local Type 3 diesel shortage. 4-6-0 No 73050 has survived into the preservation era, now being named *City of Peterborough* and located on the Nene Valley Railway. It also represented one of the new BR Standard designs at the 1954 IRC exhibition.

This scene shows a typical Reading to Redhill train of the era, with Maunsell rebuild 'E1' class 4-4-0 No 31506 together with ex-SECR 'Birdcage' triple set and van. The location is south of North Camp station on 15 June 1957 and, unusually, an isolated cattle wagon has also been included in the train make-up. The 'E1' class 4-4-0s were rebuilds of Wainwright's 'E' class engines commencing in 1919. Main alterations were firebox replacement, inclusion of a superheater, increase of boiler pressure and replacement of slide valves by piston valves. Their much improved performance made them extremely popular with crews, especially on the South Eastern section, where driver Sammy Gingell of Stewarts Lane depot was particularly renowned for exploiting their potential. Both the 'E1' class and 'Birdcage' stock had disappeared from service by the beginning of the 1960s.

*T.B. Owen*

Maunsell 'N' class 2-6-0 No 31862 gets under way from Tunbridge Wells West in April 1964 with a train for Tonbridge, having travelled over the line from Eastbourne via Hailsham and Eridge, otherwise known as the Cuckoo Line. On reaching its destination it would probably have continued as a Tonbridge to Redhill working as this was the usual pattern of operation at the time. Being a longer and slower route to Eastbourne than the more direct one from Redhill

via Haywards Heath, through timetabling was, no doubt, omitted in order to avoid confusion. The use of Maunsell narrow-bodied stock, as illustrated, was necessary because of the restricted width tunnels on the Hastings line, which were encountered between Tunbridge Wells and Tonbridge. With the closure of that section between Eridge and Tunbridge Wells West, the station and sidings area have been taken over by a national supermarket chain and accordingly

redeveloped. However, a restaurant operator has since become responsible for the original station premises, and these together with the clock tower have been retained in the new development, in much the same fashion as that at Bath (Green Park) on the former Somerset & Dorset system. A preservation society is in the process of reopening the route from Eridge, and the new owners have kindly agreed to allow the group use of the former locomotive shed as its new terminus.

*Left:* An unusual view and location for Maunsell 'W' class 2-6-4T No 31918 which is shown working an up special freight to Norwood Yard, here approaching Little Brooms tunnel, north of Edenbridge Town station on 2 March 1963. This class was more closely associated with transfer freight workings to other regions of BR, usually via the West London line. Introduced in 1931, they incorporated certain parts of the 'K' class, otherwise 'River' class 2-6-4Ts, rebuilt following the 1927 Sevenoaks accident.    *J.J. Smith*

*Above:* A pastoral scene showing the rolling country-side flanking the main A264 road from East Grinstead to Tunbridge Wells at Ashurst station, where an unidentified 'H' class 0-4-4T propels motor set No 604 towards Groombridge with an Oxted to Tunbridge Wells West push-pull working in September 1962. Ashurst was once notable as the point at which the 4.48pm evening commuter train from Victoria divided, one section being taken forward to Brighton and the rearmost portion finishing its journey at Tunbridge

Wells West. Whilst the line from South Croydon to Uckfield remains open as an extended branch, it represents the last section of those former LBSCR branches that once radiated from Eridge in East Sussex. Note the ex-LSWR box van in the station siding. A point of interest concerning Ashurst station was that, at this time, it possessed a steel fenced open signal frame mounted on the down platform, similar to that which once existed at the Sheffield Park headquarters of the now preserved Bluebell Railway.

Eastbourne station with its adjacent yard, is the subject of this view showing the empty stock of the LCGB 'Wealdsman' railtour of 13 June 1965 being removed, presumably for engine release, by BR Standard Class 4MT 2-6-4T No 80144. The yard is full of a variety of interesting EMU stock, most long since withdrawn, including a 6-PAN unit once used on London express services, together with a pair of 4-LAV sets, these having worked predominantly on Brighton to London slow and semi-fast services. A modern suburban EMU of 4-EPB type since similarly withdrawn, is also present, along with a number of loco-hauled rakes. An interesting feature is the presence of two London buses of the RT family parked outside the station. These would probably have operated one of the many garage social club excursions to various south coast resorts, that took place during the summer season.

As illustrated by this scene at West Hoathly station in July 1964, track lifting work is under way on what was later to become the Northern Extension of the well-known Bluebell Railway, between Horsted Keynes and East Grinstead. The downside shelter and footbridge here have already been removed, whilst a redundant GW tender, originally coupled to their 'Dukedog' 4-4-0 No 3217 *Earl of Berkeley*, is stabled on the former down line. This had been provided as an alternative water supply when that from the local mains system was unavailable. Former North London Railway 0-6-0T No 2650 waits to unload its cargo of track panels, probably from the Ardingly to Horsted Keynes line, in the former goods yard area of the station. The locomotive was hired from the Bluebell Railway, along with its crew, by the demolition contractors, who found their own small diesel unable to cope with the line's difficult gradients. When a boiler washout became due former LBSCR No 473 *Birch Grove*, illustrated overleaf, was employed until No 2650 became isolated north of Horsted Keynes by the lifting operations.

*Left:* In early September 1964, Bluebell Railway 'E4' class 0-6-2T No 473 *Birch Grove* is seen travelling at a leisurely pace along the rusty metals of the Ardingly branch, closed on 28 October 1963. Its load of track panels was destined for the West Hoathly goods yard recovery point. Track lifting on the previously electrified Horsted Keynes to Haywards Heath branch was under way in Lywood Tunnel, visible behind the train.

*Above:* Newhaven is depicted here, with a variety of former LBSCR tank engines present in the shed yard, during a visit by the RCTS 'Sussex Coast Limited' rail-tour on 7 October 1962. 'A1X' class 0-6-0T No 32636 is currently preserved on the Bluebell Railway as No 72 *Fenchurch* and was once the regular engine on the harbour branch, being sold to the Newhaven Harbour Co back in 1898. It returned to Southern Railway ownership in 1927, when its new identity became No 636. No 32670 is now in the possession of the Kent & East Sussex Railway at Tenterden. Regrettably, Billinton 'E6' class 0-6-2T No 32418 and 'E4' Class 0-6-2T No 32479 have not survived, although former Class 'E4' No 32473, opposite, remains as *Birch Grove* on the Bluebell line.

A general view in September 1962 of Three Bridges shed, just off the London to Brighton main line, with two of the well-known Brighton 'K' class 2-6-0s evident, along with a BR Standard Class 4MT 2-6-4T. The 'K' class was designed by Lawson Billinton, LBSCR Chief Locomotive Engineer between 1912 and 1922. Although constructed for fast freight working they could often be found, particularly in later years, on passenger duties. One such example was the Brighton to Redhill section of the cross-country Hastings to Wolverhampton working and its return journey. As a result of railway policies of the time, the whole class was withdrawn en masse, along with many others throughout BR, at the close of 1962 although completely serviceable and with many months of useful life remaining. Unfortunately, owing mainly to financial constraints, the Bluebell Railway was unable to secure an example for preservation, despite earlier plans to do so.

With Brighton station and the old LBSCR locomotive works in the background, Bluebell Railway 'A1X' class 0-6-0T *Stepney* is illustrated here at Brighton shed on 27 October 1963, close to its original birthplace. *Stepney*, together with Class E4 No 473 *Birch Grove*, had run light from Sheffield Park to Brighton earlier in the day, prior to working the 'Brighton Blue Belle' railtour on the return journey. This had been organised with the intention of giving a last run to the workmen's set of pre-Grouping coaches, used on the Lancing Carriage Works special service, before their withdrawal. In the event, this working from Brighton, known locally as the 'Lancing Belle', survived until 31 July 1964. The railtour also marked the final occasion a passenger train would be operated over the complete Ardingly branch, which closed officially on 28 October 1963. For this reason special dispensation had to be obtained to allow 'A1X' No 32636 with an ex-LBSCR milk van for the Bluebell Railway over the closed line during May 1964. It was the final working before the demolition contractors moved in.

*Below:* On 21 August 1963, against a background of newly constructed coaches, works shunter 'USA' class 0-6-0T No DS236 (previously No 30074) goes about its business in the Lancing Carriage Works of the former LBSCR, situated between Shoreham and Worthing. Fourteen of these engines, which had been designed for use in Europe by the US Army Transportation Corps, were purchased by the Southern Railway in 1946 to replace the elderly LSWR 'B4' class 0-4-0Ts which were mainly employed in Southampton Docks. Following dieselisation, many were withdrawn, but a number, including the example shown here, were renovated for departmental use in the various works and depots around the region.

*Right:* A rare view of 'Battle of Britain' class 4-6-2 No 34057 *Biggin Hill* leaving Dorking North station with the 5.13am London Bridge to Brighton newspaper train around 6.30am on 10 June 1963. This was the only regular steam passenger working north of Horsham on the Mid-Sussex line in later years, except for some summer inter-regional coastal excursions.

Two former Brighton tanks, 'E4' Class 0-6-2T No 32503 and 'E6' class 0-6-2T No 32417 leave Selham station on the line from Pulborough to Midhurst with the LCGB 'Sussex Coast Limited' on 24 June 1962. An official photographic stop had just taken place at this point. This line was then the last remnant of those previously centred on Midhurst, apart from a stub between Chichester and Lavant kept open, variously, for sugar beet and aggregate traffic. The latter was closed between Lavant and Midhurst following the derailment of 'C2X' class 0-6-0 No 32522 near Singleton, due to the collapse of an underline culvert in May 1952. The resulting recovery operation was quite complex, and aroused much interest and coverage in the railway press of the time. Selham opened in January 1872, more than five years after the line through to Midhurst was completed. With a local village population of less than 100 in 1938, passenger traffic was always light, but substantial milk and agricultural goods were handled. The yard, which closed in May 1963, was especially notable for the large quantities of chestnut fencing despatched in the interwar years. Final closure to all traffic came officially on 16 October 1964.

An unidentified 'A1X' class 0-6-0T, probably No 32650, crosses Langstone Creek with a train from Havant to Hayling Island on 2 November 1963 during the last day of normal service preceding complete closure. The bridge which, with its light wooden structure, had been the main reason for the survival of these engines, was also the predominant reason for line closure. A movable span was incorporated, this being controlled by the box visible on the left hand edge of this view. The 'A1X' locomotives were the only class permitted on the line by virtue of their light axle loading.

*Left:* The fireman drops down from the cab of unrebuilt 'BB' class 4-6-2 No 34067 *Tangmere* in order to reset the road at the rear of Fratton shed on 27 July 1963. An interesting addition to this locomotive were the cabside squadron plaques, fitted in September 1955. This locomotive was withdrawn from service in November 1963 and has since January 1981 been preserved on the Mid-Hants Railway at Ropley.

*Above:* Kensington (Olympia), previously Addison Road, station on the West London Line, at this time in October 1962, had no regular service other than that periodically provided by London Transport from Earls Court to serve the various exhibitions taking place there, and early morning and afternoon trains on weekdays, for the benefit of Post Office employees who worked at the nearby Savings Bank headquarters.

These were available for use by the general public, but for many years did not appear in the published timetable. Former SECR 'H' class 0-4-4T No 31305 is shown returning to its departure point, Clapham Junction, with the empty stock of a morning working. In the interwar years services had been provided by the SR from Clapham Junction and by the LMS from Willesden, these all being suspended in October 1940.

*Below:* In charge of an REC railtour around former LSWR suburban lines, 'O2' class 0-4-4T No 30199 is illustrated on 25 March 1962 passing the distinctive architecture of Barnes station, junction of lines to Staines via either Hounslow or Richmond.
No 30199, to be withdrawn that December, was brought from Eastleigh specially for the occasion.

*Right:* Heading a combined RCTS/SLS railtour on 2 December 1962, Beattie designed '0298' class 2-4-0WTs Nos 30585 and 30587 are shown here west of Raynes Park on their way to the Hampton Court branch. Three of these former London suburban engines had, until this time and since 1895, been mainly confined to the Wadebridge to Wenford Bridge china clay branch in Cornwall, only visiting Exeter or

Eastleigh Works for periodic maintenance or overhaul. Short-lived passenger workings between Wadebridge and Padstow were, however, known to have taken place in July 1954 and July 1962. Due to their imminent replacement by WR '1366' class 0-6-0PTs, they had been brought to London to celebrate close to a century for their class in public service. Both examples shown have fortunately been preserved.

47

*Left:* As well as visiting Hampton Court, the previously illustrated railtour also took the opportunity of visiting the Chessington branch, completed by the Southern Railway in May 1939, the train being shown near Tolworth. For this section they employed Urie-designed LSWR 'H16' class 4-6-2T No 30517, the class of five engines having been introduced in 1921 for cross-London transfer freight duties from the then new hump marshalling yard at Feltham.

*Above:* Pictured in Deepcut cutting, between Brookwood and Farnborough, rebuilt 'Merchant Navy' class 4-6-2 No 35012 *United States Lines* is seen hauling a down 'Bournemouth Belle' Pullman working in June 1966. This train had its origins in the 'Bournemouth Limited' introduced in the years before World War 1I. The inaugural service was launched in the July 1931 summer timetable, with usual haulage either by 'Lord Nelson' or 'King Arthur' class 4-6-0s.

In 1936 the 'Schools' class took over the duty, having been displaced by electrification of the London to Portsmouth route, being amongst the first engines in 1938 to wear the malachite green livery. Suspended during World War 2, the service was reintroduced in October 1946, No 21C18 *British India Line* hauling the first train. After electrification of the Bournemouth line in 1967 the service was rendered redundant, ending the Southern Region's last Pullman operation.

An unidentified Bulleid 'Q1' class 0-6-0 heads past Ash Junction signalbox on 21 April 1956 with a freight for Tongham Gasworks. This branch was the truncated section of the former LSWR direct line from Guildford to Farnham, closed to passengers when the route via Ash and Aldershot was electrified in July 1937. The line was finally shut to all traffic on 31 December 1960, when freight working ceased. On 5 October 1957 'M7' class 0-4-4T No 30051 and two-coach push-pull Set No 721 were employed on a final railtour over the branch organised by the Railway Enthusiasts' Club of Farnborough.

*T.B. Owen*

Making a rare appearance on the main system, War Department 2-10-0 No 600 *Gordon* is shown hauling an RCTS railtour from Waterloo to Liss on the Portsmouth Direct line between Witley and Haslemere on 30 April 1966. Special permission had been obtained to operate this locomotive from Guildford to Liss, from where it would take the train over the Longmoor Military Railway, its more usual territory, and then continue to Staines via the main line, providing a last working on the Bordon to Bentley branch. *Gordon* was subsequently preserved and now resides on the Severn Valley Railway.

*Above:* Getting to grips with the testing gradient between Butts Junction and Medstead & Four Marks, Urie 'S15' class 4-6-0 No 30512 is pictured with the LCGB 'Hayling Farewell' railtour on 3 November 1963. The line between Alton and Alresford is now under the control of the Mid-Hants Railway, dedicated to the memory of the former Southern Region, and possesses a variety of appropriate rolling stock, including sister locomotives Nos 30499 and 30506, both having been rescued from the Barry graveyard in Wales. At one time running from Alton to Winchester Junction, the line now terminates at Alresford. Before withdrawal of steam, services had been provided for some years by push-pull units coupled to ex-LSWR Class M7 0-4-4Ts, these being replaced by 'Hampshire' two or three car DEMUs until closure on 5 February 1973. The 'S15' class were designed by Robert Urie and introduced in 1920 for working fast freight and heavy passenger traffic, being largely based on the 'King Arthur' class but with smaller coupled wheels.

*Right:* Illustrated on the now closed section of the Mid-Hants line on Sunday 15 May 1966 is former LMS 'Black 5' No 45493 with the diverted 8.55am Bournemouth to Waterloo service passing Itchen Abbas station. The route is now severed by the nearby M3 motorway. No 45493 was being used on Southern duties as a consequence of Sunday layover between south and northbound workings of the York to Poole service. The line received the description 'Over the Alps' by enginemen owing to its difficult gradients.

*Left:* On a cold and frosty morning in December 1965, during Bournemouth line electrification works, Bulleid 'Q1' class 0-6-0 No 33006 stands in Hook station with a spoil train. A further engineers' train is visible on the up lines to the rear of the signal box. The 'Q1' class, known to enginemen as 'Charlies', was a somewhat functional though extremely powerful design introduced when wartime restrictions on the use of materials resulted in their unusual appearance.

*Above:* Rebuilt 'Merchant Navy' class 4-6-2 No 35029 *Ellerman Lines* is shown here on 5 September 1965 climbing the approach to Battledown flyover, west of Basingstoke, with a Bournemouth to Waterloo train. This well-known railway landmark was brought into use in 1897 to overcome operational conflict between trains running on the Bournemouth and West of England lines. No 35029 is of interest as it now exists as a sectional exhibit at the National Railway Museum,

demonstrating the inner workings of a steam locomotive. Unlike their sister Light Pacifics of 'West Country' and 'Battle of Britain' classes, all of these engines were rebuilt by 1959, in order to simplify maintenance, and lasted on the Bournemouth line until the cessation of steam operation in July 1967. During the last few months many record breaking runs were unofficially attempted, the 100mph barrier being, reportedly, broken on more than one occasion!

*Above:* An interesting view of 'Schools' class 4-4-0 No 30926 *Repton*, showing its various cab fittings whilst undergoing restoration in Eastleigh works in September 1966, before trans-shipment to an American steam museum. It was to spend several years there until financial problems brought its return to the North Yorkshire Moors Railway at Grosmont, an event made possible by the patronage of an English enthusiast, then working in the USA.

*Right:* An interior view of the Southern Region's main railway works at Eastleigh, where a variety of Pacific and Standard classes are seen undergoing overhaul on 18 August 1963. Note the overhead traverser crane, as well as examples of driving wheels of BFB (Bulleid-Firth Brown) patented design, as used on both Pacific and 'Q1' classes. The main works were opened in 1909 and continued to function well into the diesel and electric era, having ultimately taken over responsibility

for all the Region's general repairs, including those formerly dealt with at both Brighton and Ashford works, from 1962 onwards. Formerly, the LSWR works had been established at their original London terminus, Nine Elms, where some 817 engines were constructed, including the long-lived 'M7' and 'T9' classes. Eastleigh also possessed the largest running shed on the Southern with 15 roads and an allocation of 120 engines at its peak.

*Left:* With Cunard liners *Queen Mary* and *Saxonia* berthed in the docks area, and a variety of coaching stock occupying most platforms, 'M7' class 0-4-4T No 30376 involves itself in the duties of station pilot at Southampton Terminus on 26 June 1957. The two lines disappearing behind the left-hand signal gantry, were the access to the old Eastern Docks area. The decline of traffic through this port saw the need for such extensive facilities considerably reduced, and the line from St. Denys was consequently closed to passenger traffic on 5 September 1966.                                    *R.C. Riley*

*Above:* Former LSWR 'B4' class 'Dock Tank' 0-4-0T No 30096 crosses Canute Road from Southampton Terminus station on 6 April 1963, with an LCGB railtour from Winchester (Chesil) on the DN&S line. The figure seen on the left is that of Ivo Peters, the much respected and inspirational railway photographer, standing beside his beloved Bentley, a familiar sight, especially along the lines of the former Somerset & Dorset Railway.

The Southampton Docks area is again featured with a diminutive LSWR 'C14' class 0-4-0T standing in the Royal Pier vicinity on 26 June 1957, presumably while the crew were taking the opportunity of a quick break in the cafe opposite! The class of 10 engines had originally been designed as 2-2-0Ts in 1906 for use on railmotor services, such as that from Bournemouth West to New Milton, but were found to have difficulties with adhesion, due to their non-coupled driving wheels. Nevertheless they continued on such duties until 1914, at which time a programme of conversion to coupled 0-4-0Ts was started. Seven were subsequently sold for wartime service, mainly with the Ministry of Munitions, but three remained and survived long enough to be taken over by the nationalised system. No 30588, and sister No 30589, were often seen alongside the road traffic on the Southampton waterfront.

*R.C. Riley*

Former LBSCR 'E1' class 0-6-0T No W3 *Ryde*, bearing the intermediate Southern-based style of 'British Railways' lettering, stands at Newport (IoW) on 15 May 1952 with a railtour organised by the RCTS to cover those lines then shortly scheduled for closure. The engines located on the island were amongst the last survivors of the class, four examples having been transferred in 1932. No W4 *Wroxall* was the final one withdrawn from IoW stock in October 1960. However, a further locomotive existed in industrial service with the NCB at Cannock and Rugeley Collieries, and survived long enough for eventual preservation. Although now fitted with a non-standard boiler, it has otherwise been restored to much the same condition as when sold by the Southern Railway in 1927. It can currently be seen on the East Somerset Railway, bearing early Southern livery as No B110. The 'E1' class had been introduced in 1874 by William Stroudley, Locomotive Superintendent of the LBSCR, for use on short distance goods traffic, and the class eventually totalled 79 engines. No W4 was originally constructed in 1878 as No 131 *Gournay*, while No B110 had started life as No 110 *Burgundy* in 1877. Some 10 engines were later rebuilt by Maunsell in 1927/8 as mixed traffic 0-6-2Ts. Known as Class 'E1/R', they were intended for use on severely graded West Country lines such as Halwill to Torrington and Bere Alston to Callington.                    *T.B. Owen*

*Above:* Getting under way from Newport (IoW) station in October 1965 former LSWR 'O2' class 0-4-4T No W14 *Fishbourne*, with nameplate removed, is depicted with a Ryde to Cowes train on the now closed section beyond Wootton. The preservation society, currently operating the section between Smallbrook Junction and Wootton, is hopeful of eventually extending its line to a new site close to Newport, the original formation there now being unavailable. The pre-Grouping wooden-bodied rolling stock shown was typical of the island's coaches, until their replacement by ex-London Transport Underground stock following electrification in 1967, and were predominantly of LBSCR and SECR origin. Note also the wooden plank wagons, used for the conveyance of both domestic and loco coal. These were probably the last examples of the type employed in revenue earning service on the nationalised system.

*Right:* Awaiting time of departure with its Ryde train in August 1965, 'O2' class 0-4-4T No W22 *Brading* sits amongst the chalk cliffs encircling Ventnor station, as two enthusiasts appear to be discussing the finer points of its inside motion. Drainage problems in the tunnel cut through St Boniface Down were probably one reason why this section of line, south of Shanklin, was closed to traffic at the time of electrification. The town had one further station, Ventnor West, closed in 1952.

*Left:* A beautifully prepared 'M7' class 0-4-4T No 30060, is seen with its push-pull set of LSWR stock, leaving Brockenhurst on 28 June 1957. This local train will take the Ringwood loop *en route* to Bournemouth, at one time being the main line to its destination. Known as 'Castleman's Corkscrew', after one of the original promoters, the route was fully opened in August 1847. Closure to passengers took effect on 4 May 1964.
*R.C. Riley*

*Above:* Unrebuilt 'West Country' class 4-6-2 No 34105 *Swanage* leans to the curve at Lymington Junction on 16 May 1964 with a London-bound relief train. This was one of the last to be constructed following nationalisation. It was amongst three survivors of the batch and found its way to Barry scrapyard in Wales along with several other rebuilt and unrebuilt examples of all three Bulleid designed Pacifics. It was subsequently rescued in March 1978, and is now located at Ropley on the Mid-Hants Railway. On 3 May 1951, it was noteworthy for hauling the inaugural 'Royal Wessex' from Weymouth to Waterloo, and during the 1950s found itself frequently employed on duties over the Somerset & Dorset system. Apart from being the junction for the branch named, this was also the point at which the line for Broadstone and Ringwood also diverged. The junction box shown was built in 1888, and existed for some 90 years before closure in 1978.

*Above:* Within the heart of the New Forest, unrebuilt 'West Country' class Pacific No 34007 *Wadebridge*, now preserved, is passing Holmsley station (formerly Christchurch Road) on the Ringwood loop, with what is assumed to be a weekend London-bound main line diversion on 27 July 1963. The line was used initially until construction work was undertaken on a more direct route to Bournemouth via Sway, this opening in March 1888. Before the development of Bournemouth as a major conurbation, Christchurch had been more significant in terms of population, and Holmsley became the railhead. In 1847 this involved an eight-mile journey across heathland in a horse drawn-coach. Christchurch was eventually reached in November 1862 by a connection direct from Ringwood. It was apparently a difficult line with a number of speed restrictions, and, on opening the new main line, assumed branch line status, closing in 1935. *T.B. Owen*

*Right:* An additional strengthening coach is included in two-coach push-pull set No 609, shown here being propelled across the Hampshire heathland near Lymington Junction by 'M7' class 0-4-4T No 30129 on 27 July 1963. The Lymington branch, opened on 12 July 1858, was considered to justify electrification in the 1967 Bournemouth programme, presumably because of its ferry connection to the Isle of Wight. *T.B. Owen*

Lymington Town station with its unusual overall roof is depicted in this view, with LMS designed '2MT' class 2-6-2T No 41303 leaving on a service for Lymington Pier on 16 May 1964. The class was, precisely at this time, in the process of superseding the long-serving 'M7' class 0-4-4Ts on such duties, and is in charge of one of the regular push-pull sets. Though normally propelled in one direction, this was not possible with the substitute power which was not equipped for this method of working. The roof was removed during alterations in 1966, at which time the opportunity was taken to replace the original gas lighting. The '2MT' class was one of a number of standard designs produced in the immediate postwar period by H.G. Ivatt, at that time CME of the LMS, with the intention of replacing various elderly pre-Grouping types then existing throughout the system. He maintained this position on successor BR (London Midland Region) until 1951, and following completion of the initial LMS construction programme, these basic types were perpetuated, with variations, by BR.

With just feathers of steam escaping from the safety valves, rebuilt Bulleid 'West Country' class Pacific No 34093 *Saunton* drifts towards Sway on 16 May 1964, with an up train in the Southampton direction, bearing reporting number 253. No 34093 was in the final batch built after Nationalisation in October 1949, and originally allocated to Bournemouth depot. It was rebuilt at Eastleigh in May 1960, and was amongst those that survived to the very end of steam on the Southern Region in July 1967.

*Above:* On a warm summer's day, rebuilt 'West Country' class 4-6-2 No 34005 *Barnstaple* is illustrated near Harmans Cross on 20 August 1966, with the 11.40am from Swanage, one of the two Saturday through trains to Waterloo, run during the period of the summer timetable. The locomotive was the first of 60 rebuilt between 1957 and 1961, over half the Light Pacifics eventually being dealt with in this manner.

*Right:* Leaving Swanage terminus with a branch train for Wareham via Worgret Junction in August 1962, is 'M7' class 0-4-4T No 30379. The leading coach, No S1050S, is of interest in as much as it is a hybrid, consisting of body sections of former pre-grouping stock which were mounted on a standard SR underframe in 1927. This could often be found in use as a strengthening vehicle, on various branches in southern and southwest England, and is now preserved on the Bluebell Railway in Sussex. The line was unusual, insofar as it had survived previous closure proposals, and a diesel service using the ubiquitous 'Hampshire' DEMUs was provided until operations ceased on 3 January 1972. However, the lapse of time had provided a period in which the support gained resulted in the formation of the Swanage Railway.

*Left:* Approaching the station on 23 May 1965, BR Standard Class 4MT 2-6-0 No 76062, a former Redhill locomotive, has just left Salisbury tunnel with an unidentified working. The headcode indicates a train operating between between Southampton and Salisbury via Redbridge. This viewpoint is no longer practical for photography, owing to the subsequent relocation and diversion of the A36 trunk road in order to avoid Salisbury city centre. A concrete road bridge now exists in the immediate foreground. Salisbury was the scene of a notorious accident in July 1906, when 'L12' class No 421 heading an up American boat special became derailed at the eastern end of the station. This was put down to excessive speed through the 30mph limit as a result of crew inattention, and resulted in considerable loss of life. A memorial tablet to this event rests in Salisbury Cathedral.

*Above:* One of the best loved branches on the system was that which ran from Axminster to Lyme Regis. As a result of its extremely twisty nature, arising from the local topography, the only engines which had proved to be satisfactory were the unique Adams-designed '0415' class 4-4-2Ts. Three of these latterly worked the line until track alterations permitted their replacement by Ivatt '2MT' class 2-6-2Ts in February 1961. No 30582 is seen at the terminus on 13 June 1958.    *T.B. Owen*

Unrebuilt 'West Country' class 4-6-2 No 34099 *Lynmouth* leaves the eastern portal of Honiton Tunnel on 5 September 1964, with a pair of coaches originating from another BR region, one of which appears to be of Thompson ER-design. In the down direction, the summit of the well-known Honiton bank was reached within the tunnel, a gradient of 1 in 80 applying for most of some five miles from Seaton Junction, this presenting a considerable test for firemen on the heavier holiday trains, such as the 'Atlantic Coast Express'. Described generally as the 'ACE', this was amongst the best-known expresses on the Southern, having the distinction of carrying through portions to all the main Devon and North Cornwall coastal resorts west of Exeter, such as Ilfracombe and Padstow. On summer Saturdays its popularity was evident by the fact that the various sections started from Waterloo as separate trains. Withdrawn in September 1964, its demise was a prelude to the closure of the majority of ex-Southern lines in Devon and North Cornwall, following their transfer to Western Region control, the final section between Bodmin North and Padstow losing its DMU service in January 1967.

A general view of Sidmouth Junction on 6 July 1961, with rebuilt 'Merchant Navy' Class Pacific No 35026 *Lamport & Holt Line* on an up Waterloo main line working, whilst BR Class 3MT 2-6-2 No 82018 waits in the branch bay with a service for Sidmouth via Tipton St. Johns. Connection would be made at the latter point, with trains for Exmouth via Budleigh Salterton. The station was eventually closed on 6 March 1967 with the withdrawal of the associated branch services, proposed under the Beeching Plan of 1963. However, arising out of local pressure, following the construction of a large new greenfield estate, linked to the nearby village of Feniton, this re-opened on 3 May 1971 under its original name, using a former permanent way building recovered from the WR Minehead branch. Unfortunately, through structural deterioration, the existing station building had to be demolished owing to anticipated cost of restoration. The station underwent several changes of identity over the years, being known as Feniton on opening in July 1860, subsequently changing to Ottery Road in July 1861, to Ottery St. Mary in April 1868, reverting to Feniton in May 1871 and Sidmouth Junction in July 1874.

*R.C. Riley*

*Left:* At the Southern's main city station, Exeter Central, we see 'King Arthur' class 4-6-0 No 30452 *Sir Meliagrance* leaving the Exmouth branch bay on 29 June 1957 with what is possibly a stopping service to Salisbury. The 'N15' class, as it was officially described, was introduced by Urie in 1918 for express passenger services, and initially totalled 20 engines. Maunsell later developed the design, which finally totalled 74.                    *R.C. Riley*

*Above:* Attacking the severe climb of 1 in 36 from Ilfracombe to Mortehoe tunnel, former SR 'N' class 2-6-0 No 31831 assisting an unidentified GWR '43XX' class 2-6-0 are pictured on 13 July 1963, with a through train for Taunton via Barnstaple. This gradient was a particularly difficult task for engine crews, as it commenced virtually from the platform end at Ilfracombe, and lasted for just under three miles, only slackening in the last mile or so before Mortehoe

station. The line from Barnstaple to Ilfracombe was opened in July 1874 with the LSWR being responsible for its operation. From 1889, the GWR established a foothold, providing a through service from Paddington. During the 1950s the line saw an increase in the services provided from Taunton, whilst regular workings were introduced from Manchester, Wolverhampton and Portsmouth. Complete closure to Barnstaple took effect in October 1970.    *T.B. Owen*

*Above:* The Drummond 'T9' class 4-4-0s of the LSWR were amongst the longest surviving locomotives of this wheel arrangement in the country. Between 1922 and 1929 these were all rebuilt by Robert Urie, CME from 1912, with boiler alterations, superheaters and extended smokeboxes, producing significant improvements in performance. Known colloquially as 'Greyhounds', in latter years they were regularly seen on the North Cornwall section, before withdrawal of the final examples came in 1961. No 30729 is pictured here arriving at Wadebridge on 22 July 1960.     *R.C.Riley*

*Right:* At the far western end of SR territory, former GW '1366' class 0-6-0PT No 1368 meanders alongside the River Camel on the Wenford Bridge line towards Dunmere Junction, with a train of clay wagons on 4 May 1964. Three of these engines had ousted the almost indestructible Beattie 2-4-0WTs which have been illustrated earlier on a commemorative London tour. They were, in turn, replaced by a 350hp shunter in October 1964. By this time all clay traffic was having to be despatched via the former GWR route to Bodmin Road station. Traffic ceased completely in November 1983, thereby closing a remarkable chapter.

*Rear cover:* During the Bournemouth line electrification programme in 1966/7, to enable complete line possession, various diversionary routes were used, mainly at weekends, to avoid unnecessary disruption. In this view, taken in March 1966, rebuilt 'West Country' class 4-6-2 No 34032 *Camelford* is seen on the 1in 80 bank between Witley and Haslemere on the Portsmouth direct line with a Bournemouth-bound working.

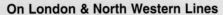